CODE YOUR OWN
PIRATE ADVENTURE

CODE WITH PIRATE PIERRE AND FIND THE LOST TREASURE

By Max Wainewright

Quarto Library

Quarto is the authority on a wide range of topics.

Quarto educates, entertains and enriches the lives of
our readers—enthusiasts and lovers of hands-on living.

www.quartoknows.com

Author: Max Wainewright
Illustration and design: Henry Smith
Designer: Adrian Morris
Editor: Claudia Martin

This library edition published in 2017 by Quarto Library.,
Part of The Quarto Group
6 Orchard, Lake Forest, CA 92630

Distributed in the United States and Canada by
Lerner Publisher Services
241 First Avenue North
Minneapolis, MN 55401 U.S.A.
www.lernerbooks.com

A CIP record for this book is available from the Library of Congress.

ISBN: 978 1 68297 182 6

Printed in China

Scratch is developed by the Lifelong Kindergarten Group at MIT Media Lab.
See http://scratch.mit.edu

INTERNET SAFETY

Children should be supervised when using the Internet, particularly when using an unfamiliar website for the first time.
The publishers and author cannot be held responsible for the content of the websites referred to in this book.

INFORMATION ON RESOURCES

You can use Scratch on a PC or Mac by opening your web browser
and going to: http://scratch.mit.edu
Then click "Try it out."

There is a very similar website called "Snap," which also works on iPads.
It is available here: http://snap.berkeley.edu/run

If you want to run Scratch without using the web, you can download it from here:
http://scratch.mit.edu/scratch2download/

CONTENTS

USING SCRATCH

In this book, we will use a computer language called Scratch to code our games. It's free to use and easy to learn. Before you set off on your voyage with Pirate Pierre, take a few minutes to get to know Scratch.

FINDING SCRATCH

To start using Scratch, open up a web browser and click in the address bar. Type in **scratch.mit.edu** then press **"Return."** Click **Try it out**.

STARTING SCRATCH

To code a computer game, you need to tell your computer exactly what to do. You do this by giving it commands. In Scratch, commands are shown in the form of "code blocks." You build a game by choosing code blocks and then joining them together to create a program.

Your Scratch screen should look like this:

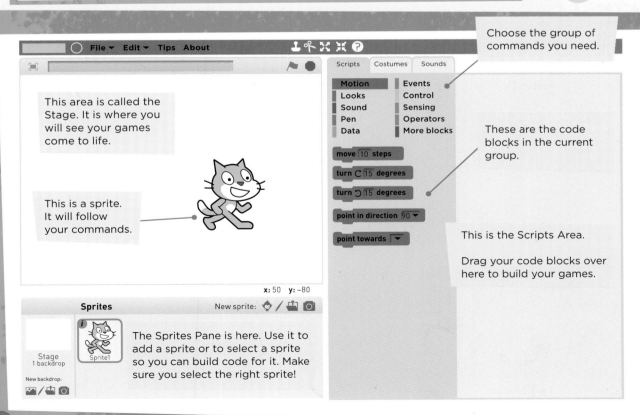

Choose the group of commands you need.

This area is called the Stage. It is where you will see your games come to life.

This is a sprite. It will follow your commands.

These are the code blocks in the current group.

This is the Scripts Area.

Drag your code blocks over here to build your games.

The Sprites Pane is here. Use it to add a sprite or to select a sprite so you can build code for it. Make sure you select the right sprite!

USING CODE BLOCKS

Before you drag out any code blocks, try clicking on one to make the cat sprite move forward...

...or rotate 15 degrees.

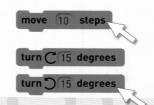

Click in the white boxes (which are shown in this book as colored) then type different numbers to change how far the sprite moves or turns.

Now try dragging code blocks over to the Scripts Area and joining them together. Click on one of the blocks to run the whole program.

You can break code blocks apart, but you need to start with the bottom block if you want to separate them all. To remove a code block, drag it off the Scripts Area.

Use the color of the code blocks to figure out which group you will find the block in. It will also give you a clue about what the code block will do.

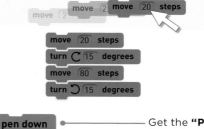

Get the **"Pen down"** block from the green **Pen** group.

The **"Repeat"** block is a mustard color, so it's in the **Control** group.

The blue code blocks are in the **Motion** group.

USING THE DRAWING AREA

To draw a new sprite, click on the **Paint new sprite** button located in the top bar of the **Sprites Pane**.

To draw a backdrop for the Stage, click on the **Stage** button located in the **Sprites Pane** then click on **Paint new backdrop** underneath it.

The **Drawing Area** will appear on the right of your Scratch screen:

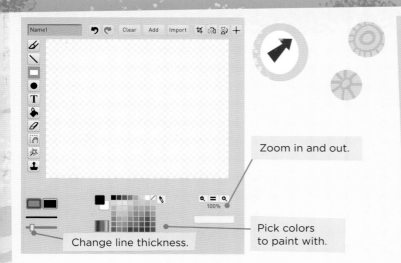

Zoom in and out.

Change line thickness.

Pick colors to paint with.

Brush
Use this tool for drawing.

Rectangle
Draw a rectangle. Hold down the **"Shift"** key to make a square.

Ellipse (Oval)
Draw an ellipse. Hold down the **"Shift"** key to make a circle.

Fill
Fill an area by clicking in it with the mouse.

You receive a message in a bottle from your old friend Pirate Pierre. It asks you to meet Pierre at the Smuggler's Inn...

You've come at last, matey. Those terrrrrible ghost pirates have been up to their old tricks! Those long dead scallywags have stolen my treasure. You must help me catch 'em on board my good ship, the *Jolly Coder*.

But shiver me timbers, you look like a landlubber! You can't set foot on board dressed like that!

Pirate Pierre is right. Before you go any further, you must disguise yourself as a pirate.

PIRATE AHOY!

1. Open **Scratch**.

First, we need to delete the cat sprite. In the **Sprites Pane**, **right click** the **cat**. On a Mac, hold the **"Ctrl"** key then **click**.

Click **Delete**.

2. To start drawing yourself, click the **Paint new sprite** button in the **Sprites Pane**.

3. Now you should be able to see the **Drawing Area**.

Choose the **Ellipse** tool.

At the bottom of the screen, click the **Solid ellipse** so we can draw a filled-in shape.

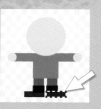

4. Select a skin color.

Draw a circle for your head by dragging the mouse in the top center of the Drawing Area.

5. Now choose the **Rectangle** tool.

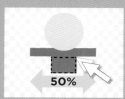

Draw two red rectangles. Make sure your pirate is about **half the width** of the Drawing Area. If not, your games might not work.

6. Use rectangles to make pants and boots.

 If things go wrong, click **Undo** and go back a step or two.

7.  Add some stripes to your shirt.

8. Use the **Brush** tool to draw your hat.

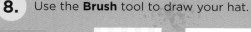

 Make the lines thicker.

 Use thin lines for the details.

 Pick **white** for the skull and crossbones.

9. Use the **Brush** tool to add any last details...   ...and make the outfit your own.

Now turn over to find out how to save your pirate drawing so you can use it on your voyage!

POLLY THE PARROT

Wait, shipmate. We can't set sail without Polly the Parrot. Go to the docks and find her!

1. Before you do anything else, save the pirate sprite you drew on page 7. This means you will be able to load the pirate sprite into other games and activities that you code.

In the **Sprites Pane**, **right click** your pirate. On a Mac, hold **"Ctrl"** and **click**.

delete

save to local file

Click **Save to local file**.

Type in **pirate** as a name for your sprite and click **OK**.

2. In the middle of the Scratch screen, click the **Scripts** tab so Scratch is ready for you to add some code to make your pirate move.

Scripts

3. Drag these blocks into the **Scripts Area**, in this order. Remember that the color of each block tells us which group it is in. So the **"When green flag clicked"** block is in the **Events** group. The blue blocks are in the **Motion** group. All the purple blocks are in the **Looks** group. The **"Repeat"** loop block is in **Control**. You can click in the white box in a block to change the message or number, so click in the **"Say"** block to type in **"Ahoy there, Polly!"**

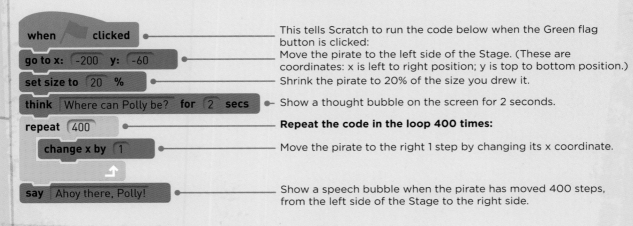

when ⚑ clicked — This tells Scratch to run the code below when the Green flag button is clicked:

go to x: -200 y: -60 — Move the pirate to the left side of the Stage. (These are coordinates: x is left to right position; y is top to bottom position.)

set size to 20 % — Shrink the pirate to 20% of the size you drew it.

think Where can Polly be? for 2 secs — Show a thought bubble on the screen for 2 seconds.

repeat 400 — **Repeat the code in the loop 400 times:**

change x by 1 — Move the pirate to the right 1 step by changing its x coordinate.

say Ahoy there, Polly! — Show a speech bubble when the pirate has moved 400 steps, from the left side of the Stage to the right side.

4. Set the background for the Stage to show the docks.

In the **Sprites Pane**, click the **Stage** icon.

Just below, click on **Choose backdrop from library**.

Choose **Boardwalk** then click **OK**.

5. To create Polly the Parrot, click the **Choose sprite from library** button in the **Sprites Pane**.

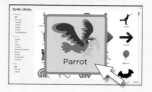

Scroll down then click the **Parrot** image.

Click **OK**.

Click on the **Stage** and drag Polly the Parrot all the way over to the **right-hand side**.

6. Click the **Green flag** button at the top right of the Stage to test your code. What happens when you find Polly?

To save your game, click the **File** menu, then **Download to your computer**. Then to play it again, you can click **File** and **Upload from your computer**.

Pretty Polly! Pretty Polly!

THE JOLLY CODER

1. Start a new Scratch file by clicking **File** then **New**.

In the **Sprites Pane**, **right click** the **cat**. On a Mac computer, hold the **"Ctrl"** key then **click**.

Click **Delete**.

2. Start drawing your ship by clicking the **Paint new sprite** button.

3. Choose the **Rectangle** tool.

At the bottom of the screen, click the **Solid rectangle**.

Select a **dark brown**.

4. Start with three rectangles.

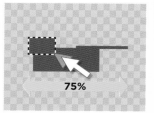

Make sure your drawing is about **three-quarters of the width** of the Drawing Area.

If not, your games may not work. Click **Undo** and try again if you need to.

5.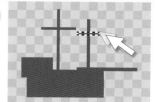

Draw four thin rectangles to make the masts.

6.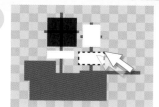

Draw three white sails and one black one.

7.

Use a thick **Brush** to round the front.

8.

Using the **Brush**, draw the skull and crossbones flag and some portholes.

9.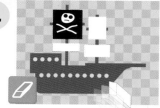

Use the **Eraser** to smooth the bottom of the ship.

10.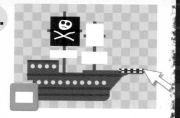

Use the **Rectangle** to add details in **dark brown**.

11.

In the **Sprites Pane**, **right click** the **Jolly Coder** sprite. On a Mac, hold **"Ctrl"** and **click**. Choose **Save to local file** so that you can use your ship later. Call your sprite **jollycoder**.

Thankee, shipmate. Away we go! Take the wheel and we'll soon chase down those ghostly scallywags.

Ghostly scallywags!

Now you need to create code to sail the *Jolly Coder* across the waves.

SAIL AWAY

1. File▾ / New — Start a new file.

2. **Right click** the **cat**. On a Mac, hold **"Ctrl"** and **click**.

duplicate
delete

Choose **Delete**.

3. In the **Sprites Pane**, click **Upload sprite from file**.

My Documents
game.sb2
maze.sb2
jollycoder.sprite2
OK

Find your **jollycoder** sprite and click **OK**.

Sprite1

The sprite will appear in the Sprites Pane.

4. In the center of the screen, click the **Scripts** tab and drag this code into the **Scripts Area**.

Scripts

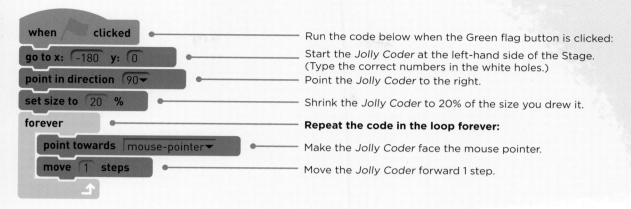

Run the code below when the Green flag button is clicked:

Start the *Jolly Coder* at the left-hand side of the Stage. (Type the correct numbers in the white holes.)

Point the *Jolly Coder* to the right.

Shrink the *Jolly Coder* to 20% of the size you drew it.

Repeat the code in the loop forever:

Make the *Jolly Coder* face the mouse pointer.

Move the *Jolly Coder* forward 1 step.

5. Now we will create a sea background.

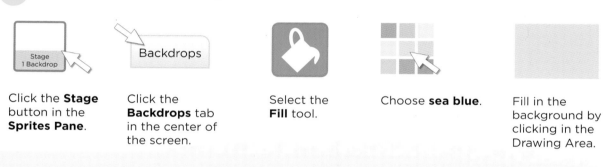

Click the **Stage** button in the **Sprites Pane**.

Click the **Backdrops** tab in the center of the screen.

Select the **Fill** tool.

Choose **sea blue**.

Fill in the background by clicking in the Drawing Area.

6. Click the **Green flag** button at the top right of the Stage to test your code. Practice sailing around. Move your mouse pointer to make the *Jolly Coder* sail toward it.

7. To save this part of your adventure, click the **File** menu then **Download to your computer**.

If I know those ghost pirates, they'll have buried my treasure in their old hang-out—Haunted Island!

WATCH THE ROCKS

Head east to reach Haunted Island. But watch out—don't run aground on those rocks!

1. Start a new file.

File▼

New

2. **Right click** the **cat**. On a Mac, hold **"Ctrl"** and **click**.

duplicate

delete

Choose **Delete**.

3. Backdrops

Click the **Backdrops** tab.

 Choose the **Fill** tool.

 Choose **sea blue**.

Fill in the background.

4. Choose the **Brush** tool.

 Choose **black**.

Make the brush width **thicker**.

 Use the brush to draw outlines of rocks.

5. Choose the **Fill** tool.

Fill in the rocks by clicking inside them.

If the color leaks out of the rocks, click **Undo** then use the **Brush** tool to fill in any gaps in your shapes.

6. In the **Sprites Pane**, click **Upload sprite from file**.

Find your **jollycoder** sprite and click **OK**.

The sprite will appear in the Sprites Pane.

---

7. Let's add a sound effect to play if the *Jolly Coder* hits a rock.

In the center of the screen, choose the **Sounds** tab.

Click the **Choose sound from library** button.

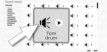

Scroll down to choose **Tom drum**. Click **OK**.

---

8. Click the **Scripts** tab. Add this code to the **Jolly Coder** to make it sail until it hits a black rock. The **"Touching color"** block is in the **Sensing** group. Drop it in the hole in the **"Repeat until"** block.

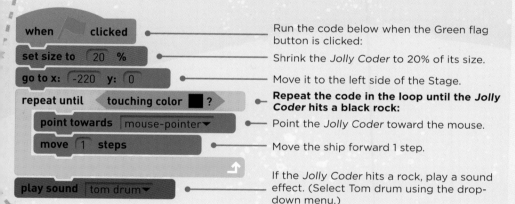

Run the code below when the Green flag button is clicked:

Shrink the *Jolly Coder* to 20% of its size.

Move it to the left side of the Stage.

Repeat the code in the loop until the *Jolly Coder* hits a black rock:

Point the *Jolly Coder* toward the mouse.

Move the ship forward 1 step.

If the *Jolly Coder* hits a rock, play a sound effect. (Select Tom drum using the drop-down menu.)

How to set the color for a "Touching" block

Click the color square.

touching color [ ] ?

The pointer changes.

On the Stage, click the color you want to check for.

The color is now set.

touching color [■] ?

---

9. Click the **Green flag** button to test your code.

Sail between those treacherous rocks until you reach Haunted Island.

To save your game, click the **File** menu then **Download to your computer**.

Finally you arrive at Haunted Island...

The ghost pirates must have hidden a treasure map around here. Let's find it! But don't get bitten by one of these poisonous crabs.

Find the ghost pirates' treasure map—but keep away from the scary crab!

1. Start a new file.

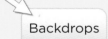

File▼

New

2. **Delete** the **cat** sprite.

duplicate

delete

3. Now we will draw Crab Cove!

Backdrops

Click **Backdrops**.

Choose the **Fill** tool.

Choose **pale yellow**.

Fill in the background.

4.

Choose the **Brush** tool.

Choose **green**.

Use the **Brush** to draw some small clumps of grass on the island.

5. Click **Choose sprite from library**.

Crab
Costumes: 2

Scroll down then click the **Crab** icon.

 Click OK.

6. Now upload your pirate sprite.

Click **Upload sprite from file**.

Sprite1

Find your **pirate** sprite and click **OK**.

7. Click the **Scripts** tab and drag this code into the **Scripts Area** to control what happens to the pirate. The **"Touching"** block is in the **Sensing** group. Drop it in the hole in the **"Wait until"** block.

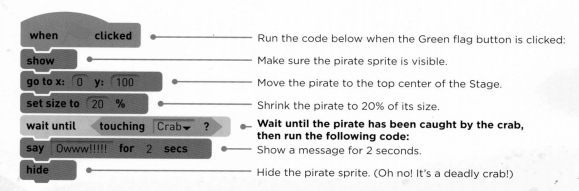

when ⚑ clicked — Run the code below when the Green flag button is clicked:

show — Make sure the pirate sprite is visible.

go to x: 0 y: 100 — Move the pirate to the top center of the Stage.

set size to 20 % — Shrink the pirate to 20% of its size.

wait until < touching Crab ? > — **Wait until the pirate has been caught by the crab, then run the following code:**

say Owww!!!!! for 2 secs — Show a message for 2 seconds.

hide — Hide the pirate sprite. (Oh no! It's a deadly crab!)

8. Drag in these 4 separate sets of code. They will make the pirate move when you press different keys on the keyboard.

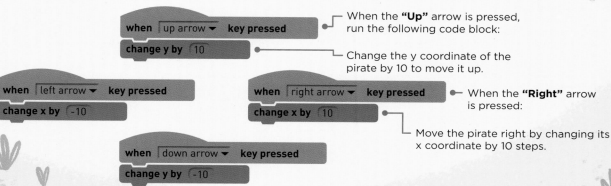

when up arrow key pressed — When the **"Up"** arrow is pressed, run the following code block:

change y by 10 — Change the y coordinate of the pirate by 10 to move it up.

when left arrow key pressed
change x by -10

when right arrow key pressed — When the **"Right"** arrow is pressed:

change x by 10 — Move the pirate right by changing its x coordinate by 10 steps.

when down arrow key pressed
change y by -10

9. Now we will control how the crab will move around. Click the **Crab** in the **Sprites Pane**.

10. Click the **Scripts** tab. Build the code below to make the crab chase the pirate around the island.

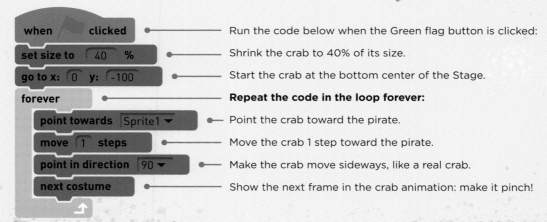

when [flag] clicked	Run the code below when the Green flag button is clicked:
set size to 40 %	Shrink the crab to 40% of its size.
go to x: 0 y: -100	Start the crab at the bottom center of the Stage.
forever	**Repeat the code in the loop forever:**
point towards Sprite1 ▼	Point the crab toward the pirate.
move 1 steps	Move the crab 1 step toward the pirate.
point in direction 90 ▼	Make the crab move sideways, like a real crab.
next costume	Show the next frame in the crab animation: make it pinch!

How the crab animation works

The animation works in a similar way to a cartoon on the TV or in a movie. By switching quickly between different images, we make it look as if the sprite is moving.

The crab sprite has two "costumes." Each costume is slightly different: one has the claws closed, one has them open. Changing the costumes quickly makes it look as if the crab is pinching!

Costume 1   **Costume 2**

11. Now we will draw the treasure map. Click the **Paint new sprite** button.

Choose the **Rectangle** tool.

At the bottom of the screen, click the **Solid rectangle**.

Select **blue** for the sea on the map.

12. Draw a large rectangle.

It should be about **half the width** of the Drawing Area. Make sure you get the size right. If not, click **Undo**.

Use the **Brush** to draw the island in yellow.

Fill it with color. (If the color leaks out, click **Undo**. Use the **Brush** to close up any gaps.)

Use the **Eraser** to make the edges of the map look old and worn.

Use the **Line** tool to add an X to mark the treasure, and any other details you like.

13. Click the **Scripts** tab. Drag over the code below to control the **map**.

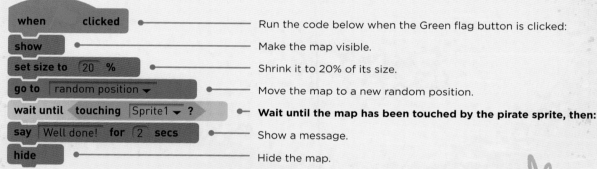

when clicked — Run the code below when the Green flag button is clicked:

show — Make the map visible.

set size to 20 % — Shrink it to 20% of its size.

go to random position — Move the map to a new random position.

wait until touching Sprite1 ? — **Wait until the map has been touched by the pirate sprite, then:**

say Well done! for 2 secs — Show a message.

hide — Hide the map.

14. Click the **Green flag** to run your code. Use the arrow keys on the keyboard to move your pirate to the map—but watch out for the crab!

Don't forget to save your game by clicking **File** then **Download to your computer**.

You follow the map to the spot marked X.
You can only see sand, sand, and more sand...

Let's get digging, shipmate! Last one to find a jewel must walk the plank.

Walk the plank!

DIG FOR JEWELS

1.  Start a new file and **delete** the **cat** sprite.

duplicate
delete

2. Backdrops

Click **Backdrops**.

Choose the **Fill** tool.

Choose **yellow**.

Fill in the background.

3. Upload your **pirate sprite**.

Sprite1

4. Click the **Scripts** tab. Drag over this code.

Scripts

when [flag] clicked — Run the code below when the Green flag button is clicked:

set size to 20 % — Shrink the pirate to 20% of its size.

5. Now drag over the 4 separate sets of code below. They will make the pirate sprite move around the island when you press the arrow keys on your keyboard. Don't worry if you haven't learned about coordinates yet. Experimenting with these code blocks will help you come to grips with them.

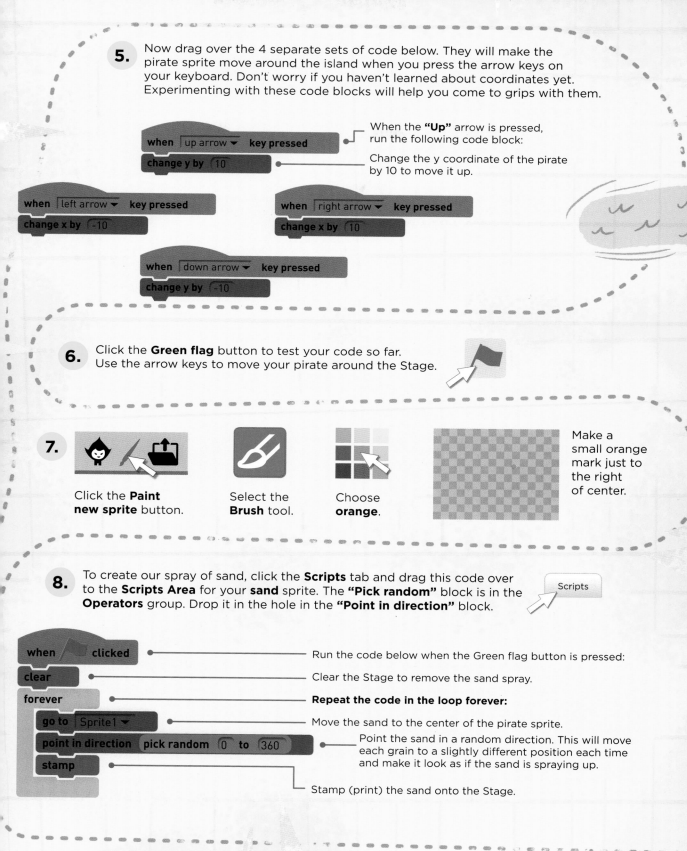

when up arrow ▼ key pressed
change y by (10)

When the **"Up"** arrow is pressed, run the following code block:

Change the y coordinate of the pirate by 10 to move it up.

when left arrow ▼ key pressed
change x by (-10)

when right arrow ▼ key pressed
change x by (10)

when down arrow ▼ key pressed
change y by (-10)

6. Click the **Green flag** button to test your code so far. Use the arrow keys to move your pirate around the Stage.

7.

Click the **Paint new sprite** button.

Select the **Brush** tool.

Choose **orange**.

Make a small orange mark just to the right of center.

8. To create our spray of sand, click the **Scripts** tab and drag this code over to the **Scripts Area** for your **sand** sprite. The **"Pick random"** block is in the **Operators** group. Drop it in the hole in the **"Point in direction"** block.

Scripts

when clicked

Run the code below when the Green flag button is pressed:

clear

Clear the Stage to remove the sand spray.

forever

Repeat the code in the loop forever:

go to Sprite1 ▼

Move the sand to the center of the pirate sprite.

point in direction pick random (0) to (360)

Point the sand in a random direction. This will move each grain to a slightly different position each time and make it look as if the sand is spraying up.

stamp

Stamp (print) the sand onto the Stage.

9. Test your code to see the spray of sand as the pirate sprite moves around the Stage.

10. Now we will create our jewels.

Click **Choose sprite from library**.

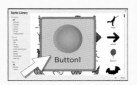

Click the **Button1** icon.

Click **OK**.

11. We need to hide the jewels when they are "buried" by making them the same color as the sand.

To do this, we will create a second costume for our jewel sprite, then color it the same shade of yellow as the background. Later, we will use our code to switch between these costumes when a jewel is found!

Click the **Costumes** tab.

Right click the **button1** icon in the **center** of the screen. On a Mac, hold **"Ctrl"** and **click**.

Click **Duplicate**.

12.

On the right side of the screen, choose the **Color a shape** tool.

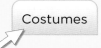

Select the same **yellow** you used for the sand.

Click the edge of the button to color it.

And click it again in the center.

The sprite should now look like this.

13. Let's create a sound effect to play when a jewel is found.

Click on the **Sounds** tab.

Click the **Choose sound from library** button.

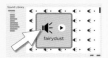

Scroll down to choose the **Fairydust** sound.

Click **OK**.

14. Click the **Scripts** tab and drag over this code for our **jewel** sprite.

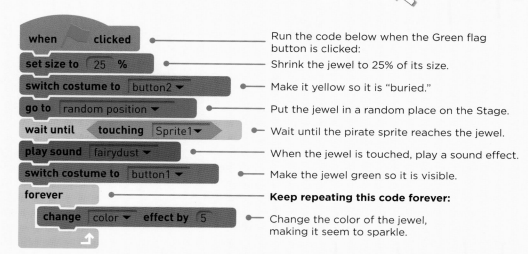

Run the code below when the Green flag button is clicked:

Shrink the jewel to 25% of its size.

Make it yellow so it is "buried."

Put the jewel in a random place on the Stage.

Wait until the pirate sprite reaches the jewel.

When the jewel is touched, play a sound effect.

Make the jewel green so it is visible.

Keep repeating this code forever:

Change the color of the jewel, making it seem to sparkle.

15. Test your code. The jewel will be hidden at first. Move your pirate around the screen to look for it. When you dig near it, the jewel will appear and sparkle.

16. **Right click** the **button1** icon in the **Sprites Pane**. On a Mac, hold **"Ctrl"** and **click**.

Click **Duplicate**.

17. Repeat step 16 to duplicate 3 more jewels.

18. Click the **Green flag** to dig up all Pirate Pierre's treasure.

Don't forget to click **File** then **Download to your computer** to save your game.

Just as you are celebrating your success, you are attacked...by the furious **GHOST PIRATES!**

We want that treasure!

Ooh-ar!

Take That!

Yikes!

GHOST SHIP

The ghost pirates grab the treasure and escape to their ship. Board the *Jolly Coder* and get the cannon ready to sink the ghost ship. Don't worry: the ghost pirates are already dead so you can't really hurt them!

1.  Start a new file and **delete** the **cat** sprite.

2. Backdrops Click **Backdrops** to create a background for our battle.

3.

Choose the **Fill** tool.

Choose **light sea blue**.

Fill in the background.

Choose the **Rectangle** tool.

At the bottom of the screen, click the **Solid rectangle**.

Add some sky at the top, using a slightly **brighter blue**.

Use **brown** to add the deck of the *Jolly Coder* at the bottom.

4. To create a cannonball, click the **Choose sprite from library** button.

Click the **Ball** icon.

Click **OK**.

Ball

5. Click the **Scripts** tab and add these 2 separate sets of code for the **cannonball**.

Scripts

when [flag] clicked ——— Run the code below when the Green flag button is clicked:

go to x: 0 y: -120 ——— Move the cannonball to the bottom center of the Stage.

when space key pressed ——— When the **"Space"** key is pressed, run this code:

repeat until touching edge ? ——— **Repeat the code in the loop until the cannonball hits the edge of the Stage:**

change size by -1 ——— Make the cannonball smaller so it looks like it is getting farther away.

change y by 5 ——— Move the cannonball up the screen.

——— **Once the cannonball reaches the screen edge, run this code:**

go to x: 0 y: -120 ——— Move the cannonball back to the bottom center of the Stage.

set size to 100 % ——— Make the cannonball normal size again.

6. Test your code so far. Try pressing the **"Space"** bar to fire the cannonball.

25

7. To make the ghost ship, we will use our old *Jolly Coder* sprite.

In the **Sprites Pane**, click **Upload sprite from file**.

Find your **jollycoder** sprite and click **OK**.

The sprite will appear in the Sprites Pane.

8. Now we will make some changes to the *Jolly Coder* as it doesn't look very ghostly. Click the **Costumes** tab.

Costumes

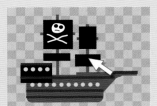

Select the **Fill** tool and choose **black**. Click inside all the parts of the *Jolly Coder*.

Use the **Eraser** to make the sails look tattered and ghostly.

9. We need the ghost ship to sail back and forth across the Stage in a straight line. To make it move in this way, we need to stop it from rotating.

Find the ghost ship in the **Sprites Pane**.

Click the **i** in the blue circle.

Sprite1

x: -51   y: 71   direction:

rotation style

Click the **arrow**.

Click the **white triangle**.

10. Let's add a sound effect to play when the ghost ship is hit by the cannonball.

Sounds

Click on the **Sounds** tab.

New sound:

Click the **Choose sound from library** button.

Scroll down and choose the **Lo geh tabla** sound.

Click **OK**.

11. Click the **Scripts** tab and move this code to the **Scripts Area** to control the **Ghost Ship**. Remember that the **"Pick random"** block is in the **Operators** group—drop it in the hole in the **"Change effect"** block.

Scripts

```
when [] clicked
set size to 20 %
go to x: -150 y: 125
repeat until < touching color [] ? >
    move 3 steps
    change ghost▼ effect by pick random -10 to 10
    if < touching Ball▼ ? > then
        play sound lo geh tabla ▼
        change color▼ effect by 25
        change y by -5

    if on edge, bounce

say You have sunk the Ghost Ship!
```

Run the code when the Green flag button is clicked:

Shrink the ghost ship to 20% of its size.

Start the ghost ship at the top left of the Stage.

Repeat the code in the loop until the ship sinks to the bottom of the screen (to set the color to brown, see page 15):

Move the ghost ship forward 3 steps.

Use a special effect to make the ghost ship shimmer and appear transparent.

If the ghost ship is hit by the cannonball:

Play a sound effect.

Make the ghost ship light up as if exploding.

Make the ghost ship sink a little.

If the ghost ship reaches the side of the Stage, change direction.

If the ghost ship sinks to the bottom, run this code: Show a message celebrating that the ship has sunk!

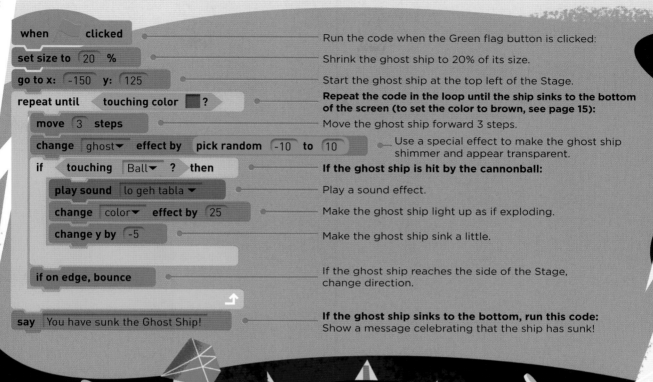

The sinking ghost ship explodes, filling the sky with dust and...Pirate Pierre's treasure!

CATCH THE TREASURE

1.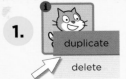
Start a new file and **delete** the **cat** sprite.

2.
Click the **Stage** icon.

Click **Choose backdrop from library**.

Choose **Beach rio** then click **OK**.

3. Upload your **pirate** sprite.

Sprite1

4. Click the **Scripts** tab and drag this code over to the **Scripts Area** to control how the **pirate sprite** moves.

Scripts

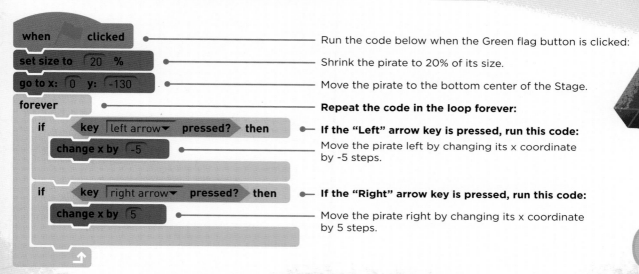

when clicked ● ————————————— Run the code below when the Green flag button is clicked:

set size to 20 % ● ———————————————— Shrink the pirate to 20% of its size.

go to x: 0 y: -130 ● ——————————— Move the pirate to the bottom center of the Stage.

forever ● ———————————————————— **Repeat the code in the loop forever:**

if key left arrow pressed? then ● — **If the "Left" arrow key is pressed, run this code:**

change x by -5 ● ———————————— Move the pirate left by changing its x coordinate by -5 steps.

if key right arrow pressed? then ● — **If the "Right" arrow key is pressed, run this code:**

change x by 5 ● ———————————— Move the pirate right by changing its x coordinate by 5 steps.

5. Click the **Choose sprite from library** button to add some treasure.

Ball

Scroll down then click the **Ball** icon.

We will use this as a gold coin.

 Click **OK**.

6. Let's create a sound effect that will play every time a gold coin is caught.

Click on the **Sounds** tab.

New sound:

Click the **Choose sound from library** button.

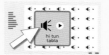

hi tun tabla

Scroll down and choose the **Hi tun tabla** sound.

 OK

Click **OK**.

29

7. It will make our game more fun if we can count how many gold coins we have caught. To do this, we will use a special part of our program, called a variable. Variables are a way that computer programs store values that can change—such as the score. We will call our variable **coins**.

Sound
Pen
Data

Click the **Scripts** tab then the **Data** group.

Make a Variable

Click **Make a variable**.

Variable name: coins

Call it **coins**.

OK

Then click **OK**.

8. Now drag this code into the **Scripts Area** to control how the **gold coin** moves and gets caught. The orange blocks are in the **Data** group. These blocks control our score.

Scripts

when ⚑ clicked ●————————————— Run the code below when the Green flag button is clicked:

set size to: 50 % ●————————————— Shrink the gold coin to 50% of its size.

set coins ▾ to 0 ●————————————— At the start of the game, set the count of coins to zero.

set x to pick random -200 to 200 ●——— Set the x coordinate of the coin to a random value. This will make it start in a different place each time.

set y to 150 ●————————————— Set the y coordinate of the coin so it starts at the top.

repeat until touching edge ▾ ? ●——— Repeat the code in the loop until the coin hits the bottom of the Stage:

  change y by -5 ●————————————— Move the coin down the screen.

  if touching Sprite1 ▾ ? then ●——— **If the coin is caught by the pirate:**

    play sound hi tun tabla ▾ ●————— Play a sound effect.

    change coins ▾ by 1 ●————————— Increase the score by 1.

    set x to pick random -200 to 200 ●— Choose a random left–right position for the coin.

    set y to 150 ●————————————— Start the coin at the top of the screen.

9. Click the **Green flag** then use the arrow keys to move left and right, catching as much treasure as you can! Your game should look like this:

Don't forget to click **File** then **Download to your computer** to save your game.

GLOSSARY

Animation – A series of pictures shown one after the other to give the illusion of movement (for example, that a sprite is walking).

Code – A series of instructions or commands.

Command – A word or code block that tells the computer what to do.

Coordinates – The position of an object determined by its x (center to right) and y (center to top) values.

Data group – The set of Scratch code blocks that control and access variables.

Degree – The unit measuring the angle that an object turns.

Drawing Area – The part of the right-hand side of the Scratch screen that is used to draw sprites and backgrounds.

Duplicate – A simple way to create a copy of a sprite in Scratch.

Events group – The set of Scratch code blocks that are triggered when particular events happen, such as a key being pressed.

If then – A common form of selection in coding, where command(s) are run if something is true.

Language – A system of commands (in the form of blocks, words, or numbers) that tell a computer how to do things.

Loop – A sequence of code blocks repeated a number of times.

Operators group – The set of Scratch code blocks that deals with calculations and comparing values.

Program – The set of commands that tell a computer how to do something such as play a game.

Scratch – A computer language that uses blocks of code to make a program.

Scripts Area – The part of the right-hand side of the Scratch screen to which code blocks are dragged to create programs.

Sensing group – The set of Scratch code blocks that detect when specific keys are pressed or where the mouse is.

Speed – How fast an object moves forward. In Scratch, we use minus speed values to move objects backward.

Sprite – An object that moves around the screen.

Sprites Pane – Part of the lower left of the Scratch screen where you select a sprite to add code to or change its appearance.

Stage – The area at the top left of the Scratch screen where you can watch your sprites move.

Variable – A value or piece of information stored by a computer program. In computer games, a variable is commonly used to store the score.

INDEX